Where Words Go When They Die

Dominic Kirwan

Where Words Go When They Die

Where Words Go When They Die
ISBN 978 1 74027 729 7
Copyright © text Dominic Kirwan 2012

First published 2012
Reprinted 2016

Ginninderra Press
PO Box 3461 Port Adelaide SA 5015
www.ginninderrapress.com.au

Contents

The Cage Maker	7
The Underside of the Tapestry	9
Reading of an Unwritten Manuscript	10
The People That Are Not There	12
Where Words Go When They Die	16
Vincent	18
1953	21
Tampon Vampire	25
The Reinvention of Cool	27
Leaving Here	31
Future Now	33
Chicken	36
Hostile Leftovers	40
Beneath the Master's Table	42
Intolerance	48
On the Same Page	50
Icarus	53
(R)evolver	56
Suicide Instruction Manual for the Damned	60
Rachelle	63
The Word Cannibals	66
Portrait of a Psychopath Unravelling	69
Tourism In the Reality Sector	71
Sanity is a Performance	74
The Indecipherable Void	77
Straightjacket Superman	78
Orchids	84
The Last Gasp	86

The Cage Maker

When they stopped feeding me
I just got stronger
I ate away the bars of my cage
Until I was free
Then I devoured the other prisoners
The guards and visitors
I filled my raging belly
With entire families
Soon I was bigger than the sky
And I rained down my shackles
Upon them all
My clouds billowed with chains
My mouth vomited handcuffs and mirrors
Over those that tried in vain
To flee

I dangled the keys to the end
Before the eyes of the cage makers
I drank the blood of God
Till he was no more than bones
In a sack of skin
Still I hungered for more
The stars withered in my shadow
I snuffed the light from suns
Like candlewicks
Pinched between wet fingers
I laughed my way through funerals
For weeping galaxies
I stole the smell from flowers
Broke the last surviving smiles of dreamers
Like twigs over my knee

When there was nothing left
Just dust and ink and emptiness
The corpses of angels
Floating dead through space
I built myself another prison cell
Got inside and locked the door
Peered out the little paper window
And waited for someone
To come along and visit me

Eons they are passing
Like echoes
Like whispers
And still I am waiting
In this nothingness
All alone inside my cage

The Underside of the Tapestry

A grim floral tapestry
Woven by gnarled, sweat shop hands
Reveals greying roses in the death throes
Viewed from underneath
It reveals nothing but mechanism
And impossible pretence
The artifice of disjointed threads
A spot of blood disregarded
From a slave's fingertip
Carelessly pierced
By someone else's needle

Yet there is more to know
More to see
In chaos and its hidden process
Than the completed image
The galleries of hum drum existence
Put on display
There is more to know
Than all the stages of the world
Can show us

Look beneath
Peer into the back stages
At the very spine of art
Pressed like lonely, broken vertebrae
Into the sweating, darkened wall
Of a living room shell
Disconnect the dots
For we are hiding there
Pluck at the exposed layers
That appear to reveal nothing
And you will see yourself
You will see me

Reading of an Unwritten Manuscript

In the first words
Of his acceptance speech
Patting his breast pocket
He thanked his pen for listening
And for always being there
He took a slug of bourbon
And choked back drunken tears
He raised a stained hand
To stem the cheering
As ink trickled down his arm
Racing like hot blue lava
From a pierced vein

In the final words
Of his rambling confession
In the space between pauses
He raised his head
To address an empty room
The scuffling feet
Of the last to flee
Echoed like the dull screams
Of trampled flowers
Murdered underfoot

A discarded apple trembled
On an abandoned teacher's desk
Several blank placards openly wept
Devastated to be left behind
They scrambled on the floorboards
Fighting over paintbrushes
And a leaking tin
Of metaphysical ink

In his last moments
Of terror
He abridged the final chapter
Summarising his life
In two, snappy, slop-culture sentences
He tore out the pulp spine of his disaster-piece
Ripped out his own heart
And mailed them both to Hell

The People That Are Not There

The bugs scratch
And the martyrs hatch
But no one hears a sound
It took some time to find you
Just to find you're not around
I can't control my headlights
Or these psycho-babble
Head mites
Can't find the road I left behind
Pass the time by dying
Drunk and blind

I'm alone
And I am lonely
But the people that aren't there
Are with me

In my little house of straw
Under the secret
Concrete floor
I left a suicide note for no one
Next to a loaded water gun
With a promise not to lie
Without a reason left to die
Or a saviour to listen
To my twisted version of their vision
Without a light to see the way
And a teleprompter script
That says I'll rue the day

In La La Land
It's time to toast
So my one glass is clinking
To the sound of one hand clapping
I will party into dawn
I will pass out on your lawn

I am alone
And I am sexy
But the people that are not there
Are still with me

The reasons are symptomatic
Like peek-a-boo traffic
They are there
If you search hard enough
They don't compare
If you call their bluff
They are delusions
And collusions
A drowning mind
And it's waving hand
To give a fuck
You've got to get one
You've got to care
To come undone

I am alone
And I am crazy
But the people that are not there
Are still with me

You've got no idea
Where I've been
What I've seen and what I've done
That makes two of us
Though it's probably only one
I give a shit
And I pray that it
Will pass into oblivion
The psychotic sights
The sickly Aphrodite
Mary Jane's on television
So don't wait up
Cos I don't give a fuck
I'm too busy making peace
With this make believe
Cardboard priest
So I'll raise my glass
Kiss invisible arse
Cos they're my friends
And I am alone
In their company
Cos they're pretend
But I'm even more imaginary

I am alone
I'm fancy free
Cos the people that are not there
Are with me

I'm entertaining
Ghostly guests
Eliminating
Graveyard pests
I'm lying in the dark
And looking through the ceiling
I can almost see the stars
And I almost feel appealing
So hurrah and hooray
For the night inside the day
But when the sun disappears
Please make certain
That you listen
With your fingers firmly jammed
Inside your ears

I am alone
It's how I will stay
Cos the people that were never there
Have gone so far away

Where Words Go When They Die

I am the monster in the corner
I control the machine
There are spiders in my eyes
Fangs in my jugular
I put them there to teach you something
But all I do is bleed

This is where words go when they die

I am the mistake in the water
Where ripples should be
There are echoes in my head
I put them there to remind me of something
But all I do is mimic myself
All I do is feed the questions
And they're so fat now
They're almost ready for the slaughterhouse
Just an electrical pulse
A prod from God
Before the throats of the herd
Are cut
To make way for the last supper

This is where words go when they fade away

I am the poison in the prison
I was injected
Into the cages of death show inmates
Hurtling through the steel eyes
Of needles

Who can say…
Whether or not I will be the last beast
They will see
Before they die?

This is where words go when they lie

I am the slack of the noose
Around the neck of an innocent man
I am the piss stain
And the warm trickle of terror
Lingering between his toes

This is where words go when I close my eyes

I am the monster in the corner
I control the machine
I wield the answers
To all of your questions
But I'm far too busy
Burying the bones
Of slain sentences
In a funeral plot twist
At night
As the cracked light
Of an oily dinner-plate moon
Mocks me
And I shovel dirt and ash and syntax
Into a shallow shadow grave

Vincent

He climbs inside
Saint Vincent's bin
Clutching stolen rosary beads
To his chest
Coughing blood
He prays the rain
Won't spoil his temporary bed
The weather report satellite
Beams information
To the brain behind his eyes
Collected by the receiver
In Vincent's secret head

In the shadow of a famous man

He's getting married tomorrow
To a headless mannequin
In a David Jones window
She's gorgeous
Silent
A little on the shy side
She'll make him a fine wife
Make him halfway happy
A devoted
Headless
Selfless bride

In the arms of a famous man

He bought her a gold ring
From a bubblegum machine
He hopes she'll understand
Now he's chewing
On the potential for romance
But the sweetness is fading
Blowing bubbles
In an op-shop can

In the heart of a famous man

In the morning he'll buy vodka
Followed by some red
He'll scrounge for durries
In the ashtrays
Of a million
Pension pay days
Drinking metho with the dead

In the soul of a famous man

Big spender!
Lashing out on used Christmas cards
From a souvenir garbage bin
To send to a family mess
That he can almost remember
For a reason to forget
He misses his mother everyday
He can't remember her address

In the mind of a famous man

Where did the good times go?
They are somewhere between the spaces
Somewhere after the holocaust
The last of the mental breakdowns
In the bottom of an empty bottle
In the hand-me-downs
Falling from the sky
All over Vincent's dust-mite bed
They are somewhere rattling
Like lucky dice
In a lonely dreamer's head

1953

On December 1953
The first production receiver
Allowing the all-seeing eye
The retina
And God's finest pupil
To broadcast reality
In colour
Was finally set free

Prior to December 1953
Our eyes were black and white
And so too, all they saw
Television and reality, it's projection
The mirrors cracked reflection
All was devoid of rainbow residue
The limits of the spectrum
Clothed in fragments
Of motion grey old movies
Wild western pictures
Black and white bullets
And dark weeping wounds

Our neighbours
Were in black and white
They entertained us
Holding parties with endless
Black and white food spreads
They complained about white noise
Mowed their grey lawns
With black and white lawnmowers

Drank black and white beer
Got drunk and forgot
The night before
The only things remembered
Experienced prior
To black and whiting out

In stark white
Straight jacket rooms
Those who thought in colour
Were rewarded, still
With black and white views
Despite their eyes
Being television screens
And their minds
Channel surfing
For a convenient way out
Of white padded hells

After December 1953
Sex was no longer
In black and white
Neither was ice cream
Pyjamas and bath robes
Absorbed vermilion shades
And pink and blue stripes
Yet sex in colour
Took a little while to recover
It was too intense
So most folks kept their clothes on
Loved their lovers dressed
In the lascivious darkness

Thank you colour TV
You allowed us all to see

When people waded
Into the lips of frothing oceans
Their ankles, sacrificial calves
Were now encircled by colour
The waters went from grey
To marine green, azure blue
And dirty brown
Automobiles adopted colours
Like crazed, zany children
Only their exhaust fumes refused
Wafting away from the new hues
To poke holes in the sky
Shooting shades of grey poison
At multi-tinted contagions
And colourful diseases
Where blood was once black
Lips were now subtle pink
And lipstick's oily smear
Made them redder, better

Thank you colour television
You brightened our oblivion

Black and white reality
Lingered in the minds
Of the old grey guard
Hiding in folds of wrinkled skin
A reminder of grey ladies
And black and white love scenes

On black and white beaches
Captured now
As we are all eventually caught
By the sky
Refracting endless oceans
That flourish in luminous eyes
Unleashed forever by the storm
That was December 1953

Black and white reality
It disappeared eventually
Now bound, are we
In exploding sheets of rain
Neon blitz bombs, longing pain
Falling under strange rainbows
The unrelenting roar of colour
And exquisite waterfalls
Of voluptuous vanity
In such a bliss as this
Nothing will ever be the same

Tampon Vampire

And the stage is mopped of my blood…
An underpaid janitor
Wearing a pink sequined tuxedo
Slops up the flood

And the television is bleached of my blood…
A fizzy blonde waitress
Guzzling effervescent manipulations
Chews on her cud

The implications of our terror
Are impossible to rationalise
The squalls of airbrushed magpies
Fill the sticky centrefold spreads
Swooping to harmonise
With a barber shop quartet
Pecking the bluest eyes
From a row of auto tune
Popped mud balloon
Splattered psychotic heads

I'm still listening
But their words now
They taste different
Somehow
Like the dying echoes
Of dead plastic heroes
Like imaginary detergent
They're spin cycle clean
A put-on display
Of affectations
And virtual dismay

Like the starched cartoon vampire
Sucking on a used tampon
In a commercial for the coldest power
He knows
Only too well
That fame is fleeting as it goes
But they're paying him by the hour

Somewhere in the world
Someone is opening a restaurant
Serving mood food
For manic anorexics
Somewhere else
Somewhere less exotic
Someone is opening a vein
With a disposable razor blade
And smiling
You should ask them about blood…
I'm all out

The Reinvention of Cool

Frank yearned to be cool
So damn cool
He wanted to be amusing
So funny that it hurt to laugh
He reached deep within himself for answers
And something brushed against his fingers
He snatched at it
His metaphysical fist sprung back
Knocking him to the ground
He held the answer in his trembling hands
He marvelled at it
With a bruised and throbbing eye:

I will not speak
Unless what I have to say
Is hysterical
I will be absolutely silent
Unless my words
Are so cool
It is worth saying them

Frank went to a party
And said absolutely nothing at all
He just stood alone
In a dark and brooding corner
And strained to look cool
He went to visit old friends
And was lost for words
They regarded him suspiciously
Put ice on his eye

He went to the toilet
Cracked a joke
Washed his hands
And slowly walked away
The sound of canned laughter
Faded from his ears
As each terminally cool step
Took him further from the flush

The days swam past him
Like goldfish
Circling a plastic shipwreck
He was horrified to discover
That his mouth had begun to shrink
His lips puckered
Retracting like a constipated kiss
His walk went from a stagger
To an irregular limp
He hiccupped his way into cool parties
Saying not a word
And slunk out of them
Leaving an air of muted indifference

He visited the toilet constantly
To practise his jokes
And to tremble
To the soundtrack of an ever cooling silence

The weeks passed slowly
Like expulsions
Of existential flatulence
He felt a growing mystery
Enfolding him
He lingered before his reflection
Pacing back and forth
Befriending the mirrors that held his cool gaze
Like the laughing faces of a frozen crowd
Held forever in a photograph

Eventually
Frank's lips disappeared completely
And his mouth recoiled
Backing into his throat
Leaving a beard of foam
A silver trail of discarded punch lines
And well-intentioned saliva

He ceased eating
Feeling it was beneath him
It was neither funny
Nor cool
Besides
It had become exceedingly more difficult
Without a mouth
He withered
Growing stick thin
His bones held court over diminishing flesh
He comforted himself with the knowledge
That anorexia was cool
So damn cool

He would have smiled
Winked knowingly at his reflection
But it was no longer feasible
He would have quipped
Lunging into a dormant
Barbed-wire wit
But that too had been swallowed
Devoured by an ever cooling void

Frank died alone
His corpse was discovered by a stand-up comedian
Draped delicately over a porcelain throne

At his funeral
In a mostly empty church
There were no tears
No one quite knew quite what to say
What to think
Or what to feel
An indifferent priest performed an indifferent eulogy
People shifted uncomfortably in their seats
The priest's final words were somewhat appropriate
'Frank…he was a cool guy,' he said.
And without thinking
Everybody began to laugh

Leaving Here

A myriad of repetitions
Plague the present sense
As it swiftly slips away
I watch him leaving
And the sadness washes over me
A lonely man in summer sleet
Dwindling between the cracks
Scarring the concrete beneath his feet
The angry jabbering of a silent crowd
Jackknifing the air before his eyes
That same panic
Dull and somehow tragic
Nipping at his ankles
Shooting rubber bullets
At a sullen target of anxiety, despair and cries
A farfetched stretch towards death
Let there be no noose!
No puppet dangling here!
Just a lonely mime to straightjacket lips
Just him seething to hold onto breath
If only the gentle strains of why
Would sketch a smile onto his sorrowed spine
If only I could hold my head so high
But I mangle rather than entangle
Gritting teeth spent within our time
Spectral memories
In a vacant dreamer's skin
Sometimes there seems no time for us to bind
The rage bubbling over in a bourbon bin

As the past passes
Through the celluloid scenes
Of a brilliant friendship
That I hope with all my heart
We have not left too far behind

Future Now

The future is now
We are all celebrities, all victims
Of glossy magazines, our faces
Airbrushed clear, invisible, to disappear,
From corporate mirror centre spreads
And scratch and sniff, phallus stiff
Modern tart motifs

Our fifteen minutes of shame
It has been extended
Indefinitely
Andy Warhol died in vain
We have thousands
Of virtual friends
We will never be alone
Our relationship status, contains us
Who's fucking who, explains us
To everyone but ourselves
We work, toiling
On virtual farms and simulations
Of animated, build it yourself
Theme parks
That we will never get to visit
Popped bubble scars
And pop culture stars
Thrive in the oily cogs, machinations
Of the nightmare factory
With long dead light, instant
Flickering as if still alive, distant
Yet thriving in the pupils

Of the blind
Eye sockets and classrooms, empty
Silhouettes of screaming,
White noise televisions
And three dimensional flat screens
Mounted on the walls of madness
By entertainment monsters
Glimmerings of truth,
Posted by cyber propaganda ghosts
Their malignant soap operas
Played out where we are hiding…
Right before our eyes

The future is now
No past to inform us
No present to get in the way
Of our narcissistic anomalies
Now is normal
Now is a twisted simulacrum
Of entities unattainable
Nothing exists any more
Not now
Not tomorrow
Not in three seconds time
Not ever
Our self-aggrandisement,
It's an advertisement
For what we left behind

The future is now
The contents of our minds, projected
Onto the wailing wall
A toothless grin drooling,
Over images of villagers
Running from explosions
That tear families
Limb from limb
Hyper-real agonies, experienced
From the comfort of vibrating
Dying room chairs
The weather is now the news
And the sky is actually falling
The evidence
Texted between textures
Of save yourself, fuck the world
Delete the goddamn universe
Self obsessed design

The future is now
And so…
We are now the enemy

Chicken

The two of them dine
In a cheap Thai restaurant
Empty of other patrons
Their minds bristle
Thinking different thoughts
Echoed in a thicket
Of nearby plastic flowers
They sip on authentic
Watered-down house wine
He does all of the talking
Rattling off work related
Ego injuries
Management machismo missteps
That he makes sound
Like bank wank victories
And puffing out his chest
Like a rooster
Temporarily bored of mounting
The other chickens
Lined up to lay
Inside his mind
Strutting around a much smaller cage
Than he would dare describe
With any accuracy
To her

When he isn't looking
She looks past him at the clock
She pokes at her choo chee
Imagines the tofu is ear plugs
And waits for a chance
To interject
And point out the strand of shrivelled
Panang-slopped noodle
Dangling from his mindfully made-up
Manicured beard
Eventually she decides against it
He looks better to her
This way

He imagines penetrating her
Up against a lamp post
On the way to the taxi rank
Like some trashy hooker
Sent down from heaven
Who it seems listens intently
To every biopic topic
Well dressed and impressed
Just so he might decide
To split a cab ride
And take her home to bed

Still, she can't see past the noodle
The smell of rank cologne
Mixes with the watery vintage plonk
And she imagines
Spilling her wine
Down his starched dress shirt
His look of horror
A priceless trophy memory
On a night devoid of laughter
She already regrets

Instead
She hurries off to powder her nose
Planning never to return
While he awaits
The unknowable certainty
Of her escape
Escapes him
He scours the empty restaurant
For other chicken dishes
And thinks again about that lamp post
Over and over
Impressed with his impression
And the minutes go by
Like snails nudged along
By sharp shovel fingernails
Oozing down his spine
Trawling through the wet concrete
Of his imagined glory

Yet soon the inevitable waiting
It becomes unbearable
He pays the bill
Ambles from the table
Cupping a shrivelled sham
Of withered testicles
Into the unforgiving night

Hostile Leftovers

Twisting on the meat hook
Of rancid charity
Mind bending maps
Guide a swarm
Of hostile insects
Up the leg of fortitude
Mandibles spasm
Like bad table manners
Drooling over the leftovers
Festering secretly
Underneath a small mountain
Of pre-chewed peas
Rejected
By the toothless party grin
Projected on the wall
Of the night before

Interruptions
In the flow of lava
Scalding the nay-sayers
And neo-Nazi pimps
Answering the prayers
Of atheists
Lepers
Pantheists
Gimps

Holding hands
With an inner volcano
As humanity soils itself
Again and again
And a sloppy version
Of somebody else's
Diarrhoea God
Changes the nappies of the damned

Beneath the Master's Table

There is an intangible difference
Between all of God's robots
In hidden haemoglobin prison cells
Writhe the wretched ring
Of insanity bells
And the corrosive clang
Of slamming doors
So it is quite understandable
For a robosexual
To languish
In anguish
In a quasi-universal parish
Crawling with mechanical laws

There are V chips
In X-branded heads
Beads of mildew shining
On prayerful foreheads
There are obligatory vomits
And compulsory carrot chunks
There are suit and tie spankers
With a Quasimodo Bible hunch

In the name of the One True Dog
And all that is evil
Clever robots
Shall waggle their tails
And stay out of trouble

There is a considerable distance
Between the floor
And the master's table
Where crumbs
And discarded lobster claws
Keep robots scrambling
Competing
Saving and deleting
On all pre-programmed fours
Devouring the scraps cast down
From a tabletop heaven

There is a bitter transience
Delusions of strained omniscience
In all of God's robots
All of them struggling
To honour the ancient laws
Of forbidden fruit
And the hunger pains
That pulse through ink veins
On a mission of contrition
With an unholy appetite
To pollute

Just one bite
And reasonable robots
Are soon fighting like children
Over the last fig-leaf
In a naked garden
From the lowest of lows
Beneath the master's table
Robots guess at the meaning
Of a meaningless fable

In the name of Sesame Street
And all that is evil
Bad robots
Shall ram-rod their dildos
Up the Tower of Babel

Perhaps
In synapse
It will all soon collapse
Debased and erased
With knees and soul grazed
Scandalised
As the paralysed
Are forced to watch
A catwalk station
Of reality television saints
In the holy throes
Of mutual mastication

In the name of the Wiggles
And all that is evil
Cautious robots
Shall cry out for redemption
And a sterilised needle

In the depths
Of the darkness
Beneath the master's table
Robots and Romeos
Juliet and Lothario
Secretly fuck
To a pornographic disco beat
Oozing from the speakers
Of God's own stereo

In the name of poetry
And all that is conceivable
Written robots shall rhyme
Most of the time
And remain largely predictable

Perhaps
In synapse
There could be time
To relax
A Sabbath
A short break
For some tea and some cake
For sanity's sake
And of course
For robotic job satisfaction

It would require
It would seem
A gastric green room
For getting some air
Letting off steam
A purgatory
With a well ventilated
Lavatory
A welcoming
Hovering
Halfway house gathering
Somewhere between the master's table
And the scum-encrusted floor

For a happy robot
Works harder
And learns it's lessons
A happy robot
Does what it's told
And doesn't ask questions

In the name of the One True Dog
And all that is feeble
Obedient robots
Shall chase after frisbees
And vacuum their kennels

So you see
There *should* be
A magnificent diversity
A malignant distance
Between all of God's robots
And it is quite okay
Perfectly understandable
For a robosexual
To lose faith
In a robotic God

Intolerance

Link me to the machine
Process my alienation
I'm tickled pink by the sickness
Yet it's getting quite ridiculous
Sleeping through the waking dreams
Of insecure supremacists
On reality medication

(Insert tolerance here…)

It's invitation only
Yet it's getting kind of lonely
At a funeral for ringing phones
Defined by loss and…
Fairy floss and…
The steady hail of stones

(Insert persecution complex here…)

Behold the blind visionary
With a voodoo doll
Pierced by bowling pins
Behold the popcorn messiah
With a punctured lung
And packet pasta grin

(Insert paranoia here…)

Surgical dissection?
It's almost credible
Wading neck-deep
Through the salad swamps
Of slave fiction
And bobbing like a vegetable

Behold the quicksand clown!
Deep below
Yet looking down
As the wheelbarrow charmer
Mixed-emotion farmer
Rolls the bullet ridden corpse of sanity
Right through the centre of town

(Insert applause here…)

On the Same Page

Look at these words
They write themselves
Listen to the ink
The murderer's song
The readers think
They know themselves
Sad to say
They're wrong

A crippled scrawl
In a paper hole
Circus mirror
Tricks your eye
Strange how the readers
They do crawl
Strange how the words
They die

Dancing in circles
Brings you back to the start
The scribe in the scribble
Will break your own art

So splendid to draw you in
Welcome to the soul cage
The page you're living in
Gather up your nightmares
Things will be just fine
There are certain clues
To comfort you
Between every fucking line

Punch the keys
With your fists
Shove the meaning
Up your artifice
From rage to stage
To shallow grave
As you are reading this
It too is reading you

Ink-stained lips
Kiss blackened fingertips
There is no point
Looking to the sky
If you wish to know of heaven
The visiting hours
In Hell
Extend beyond goodbye

This truth is the whitest
It's sharpened teeth
The love beneath
A bright and snarling lie
Little gestures breeding
Like nervous ticks
Tiny meanings feeding
On gesticulation tricks
All hail
They shape a well trained
Muddled mind
If you take away the words
Reality is left behind

Look at this hand
It paints the ending
Look at this skin
It crawls with meaning

Look at these lines
For they are prison bars
Remember these rhymes
They are death scars

It's a violation
Of the rules of the game
Poisoned ink pumping
Through psychotic veins

Look at this face
This oblivious shell
Creep behind these eyes
You know them well

Icarus

The stench of burning feathers
Fills the luminous I
Smoke billows
Spewing shadows
From the mouth in the sky
Stinging the engorged retinas
Slaying the ill fated messengers
Fleeing from this being
The one true dog
With singed waxen wings
Dividing fear from faith
Engulfing the ascension
In septic smog

Rubber bullets ricochet
Off snoring robots
And the pungent sullied fur
Of crucified rabbits
Over my bough and brow
I creep
Toward an impossible horizon

Poisoned lips
And silted claymation tits
Tongue the hollowed cheeks
Of misanthropic misadventure
I am somehow alive
Doomed to stagger
Irregular limp lampooned
Under cascading waterfalls
Of unhinged laughter

Filling the unfillable prescriptions
The drunken misdirections
Of the finally sober

Free to wander
Across the drool slopped stage
Free to savour the invisible Saviour
Dangling before a carrot stick grave
Snapping and gnashing
With pale picket fence teeth
At the keys to the endgame cage

I am anything but over
The nothingness that beguiles
This knowing now
Fills my eyes with filth and faith
If the pariah messiah
Would allow me the grace
I could write my way
Riddle myself
Out of this place

From tepid fictions and liquid demons
I would rather corrupt
This cancerous bubble
Than drink the ink
The black blooded ooze
That weeps from these wounds
Than pour one more drink
Into the deplorable well
The deepest death hole
And shed yesterdays bloated
Drunken hell
For a soul

(R)evolver

It's impossible for him to speak
With the barrel in his mouth
But he tries
His prayer comes on
Like a tearful, gurgled eulogy
And as she listens to him, intently
She smiles that smile he knows
She drags on a cigarette
She flicks ash
Into the tear stained carpet
Moisture gathers, like wine
Between her legs
He attempts to grin back
But cannot
The cold, steel barrel
Deep throated, wedged
In wordless, crazed woe
That one solemn, lipstick-coated bullet
That she kissed
Like an unborn babe
It remains nuzzled in the chamber
Of the revolver
In ruinations womb

Every click
Is an uncoiling viper
A memory edging closer
To the end of all his memories
The trigger is slippery,
Oil and sweat mingles
Like battery acid and spring water
Meant to be together

His eyes are ravens
Clawing and screaming
With vein streaked shrieks
His dark pupils perch in hers, searching
For permission to cease
To stop this
'Go on,' she nods
Moving closer
She slowly unzips his fly
Then another click
Another gurgled, echoed prayer
Another grab at silence
Dismissed
The hammer of his pulse
His neck vein throbbing
Blitzes out all reason
Muting what should be indifference
Replacing death and lust
With the tightening noose
Of panicked sorrow
Then…the third click
The fourth
He is in her mouth now
She is no longer watching
She devours him
He pulls the gun out of his throat
He coughs, splutters, moans
Whispering coldly, he urges,
'Go on…'
And lowers the barrel

Pressing the point, delicately,
Deliberately
Into the top of her head
Slime and saliva glisten
Catching improbable light
From a dim bulb, swinging
Phlegm falls from the barrel
Like spider's web
Mingling with her hair

Click…
She stops
Frozen, listening
But she does not look up
There is only one chamber left
One unexplored cell
In their asylum
In a cheap hostel
On the edge of nowhere

One shiny, sheathed bullet
Slicked thick
With blood-red, goodbye lipstick
Cries out for a killer, a deranged lover
For a chance to shatter bone
To pierce skin, to rush uninterrupted
Through supple flesh
Weeping for unconscionable death
And for madness,
Such sacrosanct desire

It is the bullet itself, sentient
Demanding release now
Hungering for what comes next
But will it get its way?
In love…
Is this the way every game must end?
Silent, vulgar and unspent?

Across the hall
In an adjacent hostel cell
A sudden explosion, deafening,
Unexplainable
Tears a hole in folds of night
Waking an old drunk from his slumber
A disturbing dream, half remembered
Lingers in the drool
Of his moist, soft pillow
He mumbles angrily to himself
Something about curfew
Something about the rules
Then he turns over
And over and over and over
The sound, ringing, fades from his ears
And ever so soon
Unknowing and too fucked to care
His eyelids close,
Slow like velvet, wrinkled curtains
Over an unseen matinee
And he too drifts, far away
Into the untold dark

Suicide Instruction Manual for the Damned

Planets collide
Worlds implode
Another schizophrenic
Alcoholic
Devours their own navel
As the tide
Reaches up to swallow
Another drought stricken
Neon street

Drugs get popped
Like minds shot
Riddled with arrows
From Cupid's wayward bow
Another Viagra victim
Goes on a killing spree
Bullets pulsing
From diseased guns
Into the foreheads
Of the uninfected
Like identity chips
Injected into the willing veins
Of unwilling babies
Taught to bear
The mark of the priest
Baptised by an evangelical capitalist
And raised forevermore
To live that way

The corporate media
Hosts another fancy press
Lie fest
And we're all hooked
And over-dressed
For the show
No one can tell you how to live
But there are suicide
Instruction manuals
Available for legal download
On the internet

No one can explain God
But everyone sees him
In the mirror
He's even caught in the eyes
In the irregular beat
Of an atheist's heart
He is…she is…we are…
And no one will ever know
For certain
Where we'll end up in the end
We just know that the remote control
Remotely controls us
The television can read our minds
Because it programmed us
To think this way

No one knows how to build
A cathedral
That welcomes every faith
But you can download
The manual
For making a bomb
That would blow it up
On the world wide web

Soon
The death toll will be jinglified
The statistics put to music
So we can dance
And shake our booties
As the end of lives
That mean nothing
When the world is dying
Are reeled off
Like the scratched records
Of an in-humane history
Like burnt CDs
Trapped in burning buildings
Crying out for the very real toll
Of imaginary Wars
For temporary
Capital-jism profits
To just stop
As if that's all anyone
Anywhere
Ever really wanted
For it all to stop
Stop
Stop!!!

Rachelle

When I think of this failure
I see an ashen rainbow
Burnt to the ground
Like it never left it
Like it ever could
I remember pursuing something spectral…colourful…
That could only ever end in darkness

You entered my line of vision like a beautiful wound
Oozing life and suffering
Pissing pain and crazed memories
A series of unpredictable cancers washed over me
Drowning my sparks and enlightening them still
All at once I was alive
Yet still
Smashed against a concrete wall
Where the tide meets the end of the sand
Where the beach was swallowed
Disintegrating into a solid void
Covering some stupid sense of desire
Some pathetic self-solving riddle
That awakened my wanting
And like every other dimwit with only half my will
I failed
My retarded charm and chaotic laughter disappeared
My bloated wanting died over and over
My clumsy desire suffocated
Under unrelenting waves of your disinterest
I was marooned by the impossibility of your longing
Like a crappy pulp romance
That nobody else will ever understand

Like the use of the word like…
Like…
Like…
And its useless applications

The story revealed itself
In timeless blunder after blunder
A cordless television
Saccharine pride and insanity
Plundered by a love
That had nothing to do with anything real
I have been delayed by imaginary histories
All night reveries
I have fallen in love
With my best friend
The last person I ever wanted
The last woman it seems
I ever will

I am captured by comfort
Now
Like the final chapters
Have written me into oblivion
How am I supposed to sever this limb?
I can barely write about it
How am I supposed to move on?
When I am caged by the very things I sought
When I cannot stop crying
When I feel like I am dying
What have I now
But trust and inconsolable regret?

What am I left to love but triumph over madness?
I have learned more of passion
In your temporarily temporary embrace
Than I could ever have hoped to know

What sort of fool am I now…
To only feel the cold?

The Word Cannibals

The heat of the light
Engulfing one, who got too close
To the truth, tumbling
Like loaded dice
From the great casino in the sky
Coming down
Raining fire and bones
Till there is nothing left
For us
But scorn and scars, deepening
Electric chairs, glowering
To fry and then flay flesh
As monsters lock lips, and kiss
With tongues probing mad mouths
And magic ritual-isms
Performed by rabid dogs
And shamans
Without shame nor a shovel
To dig the right grave
For the right-sized cadaver
For the right memory, lost
In a bee hive mind

The swarming of saints and ants
Overwhelms the gates
Of cities, disrupted by salival skies
Drooling over the lovers
And the leftovers
Of a dinner party diorama
Starring approximations of Gods
Made from matchsticks
Tarot cards and naked, shaking flames

And then more fire…
And then more bones…
Burning truths and absolutions
Into the foreheads of the word cannibals
Shrieking, mad with desire
Lost in mazes made out of mouse skulls
And blue screaming cheeses
Tempting true disbelievers
Till nothing
And then more of that same nothing
Compounds a cartoon abyss
Where emissaries of mission
Throw themselves off heathen cliffs
Into oncoming traffic
On motorways and arterial pathways
Looking for the quickest way to the brain
Of the last lucky caller
On a radio
Mind map game show
Where everything is shrinking
And megaphones
And microphones
Broadcast hatred for those hated
And leave me alone,
Pelted by petals and then stones
With lavender incense tones
As Capital-jism digits
Splayed like webbed fingers
With nails driven home
Into wrists and after being out

All night
By insane sane-ists
And escape artists
Every word eaten
Devoured by sullen words spoken
Every step closer
To the truth of psychotropic yesterdays
An aggressive cancer
Enveloping a wounded stranger
Bound by regret
And riddled by carnivorous bullets
On the edge of reality
Estranged by the word cannibals
Those who would stop at nothing
Those who would eat even themselves
If it meant another chance
At saving their sunken
Invisible faces

I now cower in fear
Before a statue, a version
Of another person
Who used to be me

Portrait of a Psychopath Unravelling

One word
Crying out for blood and ruptured spleen
One tear
Rolling down the face of the devil
All of these mind crimes
Unseen

And I told you that I don't care
And I told you
That my emptiness would set you free
And I told you a lot of things
But you were never really there
Absentee
A know-it-all show
Aghast, a reality refugee
We should build a bridge over this river
My eye's membrane,
Filaments, bursting at the seams
With cum and rum and rancid nicotine
Even in the darkest hole
I can still hear your silence
Even in the pig pen
I can breathe and bathe
In the mud and ooze
That pumps from your heart
Like entrails
Dirty and irredeemable
The pulse of succulent flesh
The stench of Messianic wine
Spilt like guilt, all over me

So let the maggots go free
This is the last time
The first time
The only time
Yet still I cannot see

This door frame, collapsing
These cracked, migraine windows
Are the eyes of a raped God
They open and close
For fickle crowds
Of maniacs, masturbating
To ghost pornography

I laugh
Like a wall
Like a descending ceiling
Like a prison cell, shrinking
Closing like a slave's shaking fist
In protest of love
One finger at a time
Over a crumpled sketch
An artist's rendering
Of my very own Armageddon

Tourism In the Reality Sector

This bum on Bourbon Street
A toothless grinning drooler
Armed to the quivering legs
With a sales-pitch cackle
Said unto me
'Buy my snake oil!'
I handed him a cheap cracked mirror
He smiled like an unemployed Hollywood extra
Gave me a vial
I took a long and inconsiderate slug
My eyes crossed paths
And two intrepid pupils
Eager to learn
Followed a rat up the drain pipe of despair
It got immeasurably dark
The air suddenly thickened
As lashings of dreamlike flatulence
Flattened the void
All of a sudden science chimed in
And hundreds of little white men
In little white coats
With microscopic microscopes
Proclaimed at the top of their tiny voices
'The world is no longer a pancake!'

Right about then
I realised something was very, very wrong
The snake oil had scalded my tongue
Writing words
Where words shouldn't be

Now
When I poke it out
My ink-pink tongue
You can read things there
Things like
'Mmmmmmm…death is near.'
Or
'I like the aftertaste of sorrow.'
And
'Licking is my business…
And business is good.'

I have since decided
To forgo any further transactions
With bums
Snakes
Drain snipe rats
And oily tattooists
I've also decided to forgo
Eating pancakes
And participating in reality experiments
No matter how real
And so I shall ignore
The insistent rapping
Of madness tapping
Upon my door
In favour of reruns of a fictional life
And imaginary dictionaries
That re-define the words
Permanently inscribed
Upon my tongue

If I keep the words trapped
Within my mouth
Their true meaning
Will always remain mine
And mine alone
And I can relax
Do some interplanetary travel
Perhaps
Maybe get a fake tan
Make a mockery
Of what not to do
Savour the summery taste
Of the rings of Saturn
As all good galactic tourists should
After all
I hear it's lovely there
This time of year
And I sure could do with a really long holiday
From myself

Sanity is a Performance

Outside the nut house
Everybody is crazy
They just do what they're told
Walk
Like they're expected to walk
Cry
Like they've seen people
On the television do
Kill
Just like in the movies
Work
Like it looks like they're working
They're well trained
These thinking monkeys
Their sanity is a performance
Timed to perfection

Inside the nut house
It's the same as outside
Except people don't know how to act
Their walks are limps
Their job is to swallow pills and sleep
Without killing anybody
They can't cry
Because the needle in their arse
Has siphoned away
All of their television tears

I hide in the halfway house
I know how to act
I know if I walk as normally as possible
Without drawing undue attention
No one will lock me up
My job is to write poems like this
To explain myself to me
But when I cry
The television drowns
Under cascading waterfalls
Of unchecked emotion
The power goes out
Temporarily
And I stab myself in the head
In the darkness
Over and over
With a plastic fork

And when I die
I will act pretty much the same way
I'll just go from moving slow
To not moving
By the time it comes around for me
The television will have been swept away
Eons ago
There will be no tears
As no one will remember how to cry

And in my open casket
I will be smiling
Just like I bribed the guy at the morgue
To make me
To manipulate my lips
To airbrush away my mistakes
My psychological acne, my horrors
A life of grinding teeth
Like the pickets
Of an old rickety fence
That keeps nothing in
And nothing out
Wiped out of existence
Torn from the suspiciously moist pages
Of a bland, well performed history
And the people
They will think I was happy
Truly happy
Like they're supposed to

The Indecipherable Void

In the awakening mind
Milliseconds pass
Like timeless bubbles
Frothing in the wind
Lost in thoughtlessness
In a forgotten fish bowl galaxy
As rotting god-flesh monsters
Swim through plastic shipwrecks
Insignificant dream deaths
Engulf the strolling reality tourist
Swirling all around the emitted light
From dark-don't-matter particles
Sharing unknowable regrets
They gather together
Yet remain apart
Other than the others
Yet the same in every way

On this checkered table cloth
Each ancient stripe
Might as well be a prison bar
Beautifying a cage
Built to hold a pickled mind
On a stage that stages atrophy
To rounds of piss and vinegar
Each shout
Drowned out
Poured down a drainpipe gullet
As canned applause
And laughter so cacophonous
It would make deaf ears bleed
Flattens and fattens
The indecipherable void

Straightjacket Superman

1

There is no one else
In Heaven
Just me, myself and mine
The neon void
Is sparkling
Like a fine white wine
I've got a date with delirium
And I am having a…
Super
Duper
Time

There is nothing much to do
In Heaven
Lexicon Luther is downstairs
If I could locate the Daily Planet
It would be the answer to my prayers

Flying through the emptiness
Sex appeal on stun
Doesn't matter that I'm bulletproof
No criminals
No guns

I'm the only superhero
In town
A bounder
Cad and clown
Yet I'm yawning
It's getting boring
For the schizophrenic king
Without a crown

I'm faster
Than a flushing toilet
Louder
Than a silent sound
I can leap tall
Psychiatric assessments
In a single sullen bound

My red cape is fluttering
My super mouth is spluttering:

Now where's that phone booth?
I really need to change
Where's Lois?
It's time to rearrange

Look there!
Up in the ether
It's a bird
It's disdain
It's someone else to blame
Will it be this way forever?

There are saints
Of all kinds
In their version of Hell
Out of their minds
And there's no one they can tell

Imagine
Mahatma Gandhi
Spanking Germaine Greer
Imagine
Mother Theresa
Pursuing a Hollywood career

There are cripples
Healing martyrs
There are ways
Of curing laughter
No Night Owl
No 7-11
There's no convenience
Here in Heaven

2

There is no one else
In Hell
Just me, myself and mine
The flames are ticking
The clocks are melting
There's no way to tell the time

I need to know
Who is responsible?
For starting this damn fire
I want to know
How to be beautiful
And the surgery it will require

I would complain
But I'm insane
And I'm getting quite a tan
I'd slip slop slap
But I'm almost black
And I feel like a new man

Red and yellow spandex
A tapestry of Lycra blue
I have X-ray vision
A version of oblivion
But there is no one to see through

The black and white
The cartoon pain
Bleeding together
In the psychotic rain
My heart is slowly turning gray
A mild-mannered reporter
Stole my spectacles
Ripped my identity away

My cape is burning
I can't out run it
Doesn't matter how fast I go
The Devil is a liar
Says don't question the fire
Says I should grin
And go with the flow

But my mind went wandering
It hasn't come back
My lips are blistering
I'm hooked on crack

Now where's that phone booth?
This is no way to behave
I can't find Lois
And there's no one here to save

This frequent flyer miracle
Merely makes me want to drive
I'd use Hell's public transport system
But I might not get out alive

There is a telephone
Ringing in my head
I'm pretty sure it's Jesus
Dialling from the dead

I promised if I got back
I'd bring him cigarettes
He swore that he was quitting
The nicotine is winning
Some halos light up after sex

There's no one here in Hell
In Auschwitz
Or Berlin
Hitler left for a bar mitzvah
And there's no way
I'll be letting him back in

3

It's so lonely being Superman
In Heaven and in Hell
Thanks to reincarnation
There's no one for me to tell

I should look
On the blight side
I'm still the man of steel
Except there's nobody to rescue
And no other way to feel

4

There are straightjackets
Custom made
For every wayward hero
There is an intangible thrill
That gets waylaid
As we count down the ways to zero

Orchids

Resentment
The love it doth murder
Another dream goes missing
And I can feel the petty hostilities
Resting like vultures in your eyes
They gather like drunken orchids
Flexing petals and sharpening a beak
That churlish monsters would not abide
Ready to pounce on me
My whirling dervish
My karmic surrender, lavished
With mindless splatter
These silences, once peaceful
They are now screams
These grudges, climaxing
Like the awkward orgasms of a fiend
Like rabid addicts
Foaming from the eyes
For that final fix
The one that will mend everything

I mislaid my heart
In a storm
Of jagged brambles and thorn
My mind weeps
A vintage red wine
That would be blood
If only I could retrieve the valves
The arteries and the compunction
To pump it
But the wraith's of wrath
Have got to the bitter seed in me
And I have no more to give

The Last Gasp

Stay calm and collected
Try not to shake
Hold on to the memory
In the deepest depths of space

Loneliness is sacred
It is all you will ever know
A fiendish sunrise
With a scorched earth afterglow

Suicide
On your side
Inside a martyr's cage
Withered from the wondering
The last words raw and trembling
Torn from the final page

www.ingramcontent.com/pod-product-compliance
Lightning Source LLC
Chambersburg PA
CBHW070049120526
44589CB00034B/1680